KT-479-436

Please return on or before the latest date above.
You can renew online at *www.kent.gov.uk/libs*
or by telephone 08458 247 200

551.45

CHARTER MARK

CUSTOMER SERVICE EXCELLENCE

Libraries & Archives

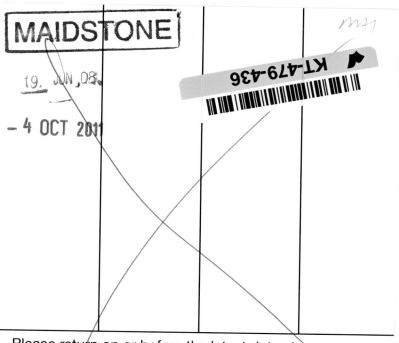

Kent
County
Council

00884\DTP\RN\07.07   LIB 7

GEOGRAPHY FILES

Coastlines

Gianna Williams

WAYLAND

GEOGRAPHY FILES

First published in 2007
by Wayland
This book is based on *Geography Fact Files: Coastlines* by Michael Kerrigan originally published by Wayland.

Copyright © Wayland 2007

Wayland
338 Euston Road
London NW1 3BH

Wayland Australia
Hachette Children's Books
Level 17/207 Kent Street
Sydney, NSW 2000

Produced by Discovery Books

Subject consultant: Keith Lye

Illustrations: Michael Posen

British Library Cataloguing in Publication Data
Williams, Gianna
Coastlines. - (Geography files)
1. Coasts - Juvenile literature
I. Title
551.4'57

ISBN 978 07502 5270 6

Printed in China.

Wayland is a division of Hachette Children's Books

Acknowledgements

We are grateful to the following for permission to reproduce photographs: A1 Pix 3 top (Superbild), 3 middle (Claes Axstal/Superbild), 11 (Superbild), 16 (Claes Axstal/Superbild), 36 (Superbild); Alamy back cover left (Bryan and Cherry Alexander), 5 bottom (ImageState/ Pictor International), 9 bottom (Buzz Pictures), 13 top (Chris Gomersall), 15 top (Doug Steley), 23 bottom (Robert Harding Picture Library), 28 (Bryan and Cherry Alexander), 29 (Steven Allan). Corbis 6 (Jonathan Blair), 8 (Bettmann), 10 (James L Amos), 17 (Michael Busselle), 20 (Jason Hawkes), 21 top (NASA), 31 (Lowell Georgia), 32 (Tiziana and Gianni Baldizzone), 34 (Bill Ross), 37 (Dave Bartruff), 45 top (Philip Wallick); Eye Ubiquitous 1 (Tim Hawkins), 19 bottom (Tim Hawkins); FLPA 5 top (D Fleetham/Silvestris), 25 bottom (T Fitzharris/Minden Pictures), 26 (E and D Hosking); Hutchison Library 3 bottom (Bernard Regent), 18 (Bernard Regent), 40 (Bernard Regent); James Davis Worldwide 33 (James Davis), 42, 43 top; PA Photos 41 (EPA), 43 bottom (EPA); Nature Picture Library 7 (Rick Price), 12 (Michael Pitts), 24 (Tony Heald), 27 (Tony Heald); Photodisc Collection front cover (Getty Images); Rex Features 4 (Richard Austin), 30 bottom (David Lane/PBP); Science Photo Library 13 bottom (NASA), 25 top (Dr Gene Feldman/NASA GSFC); Still Pictures 15 bottom (Nigel Dickinson), 21 bottom (Fred Bavendam), 22 (Bojan Brecelj), 35 (Reinhard Janke), 38 right (Mark Edwards), 38 left (Hartmut Schwarzbach), 44–45 (Schalharijk/UNEP), 45 bottom (Hartmut Schwarzbach), 47 (Bojan Brecelj).

Contents

The words that are explained in the glossary
are printed in **bold**.

Introduction

The coastline is where the sea meets the land. There are many different kinds of coastline.

Constant change

Coastlines are constantly changing. Each day their shape is changed by the tides as they rise and fall. Other changes happen more slowly, over thousands of years. Earthquakes and volcanoes can raise or lower large hunks of rock. The shore can become jagged or smoothed over. Pounding waves wear away the land in one place, then pile up new land at another. Winds scoop up sand and heap it into **dunes**.

▼ Giant waves pound England's Dorset coast, and are dangerous for people and buildings.

 **Fact file**

Coastline lengths

The biggest countries don't always have the longest coasts:

Canada	243,791 km
Australia	25,760 km
Norway	21,925 km
United States	19,924 km
United Kingdom	12,429 km

Coastline measurements aren't always the same. Norway's coastline is only 2,650 km if inlets and bays aren't measured.

▲ The clear waters of this Indonesian coral reef are teeming with life.

Natural wonders

Every natural coastline has its own special mixture of animals and plants. In warm water, coral reefs may develop. These are home to some of the world's most exotic and colourful sea animals. Even the rock pools of cooler coasts can be home to many different creatures.

A home for people

People need the coast too. The sea is an important source of food and a way of travelling. But often people use the sea as a dump. Many of our coastlines are badly polluted. Sometimes the sea is not even safe to swim in.

▼ Sun, sea and sand – visitors to California's Venice Beach enjoy all three.

Fact file

How far we are from the sea

Distance from sea (km)	Population (millions)	Percentage of population
up to 30	1,147	20.6
30-60	480	8.6
60-90	327	5.8
90-120	251	4.5
over 120	3,362	60.5

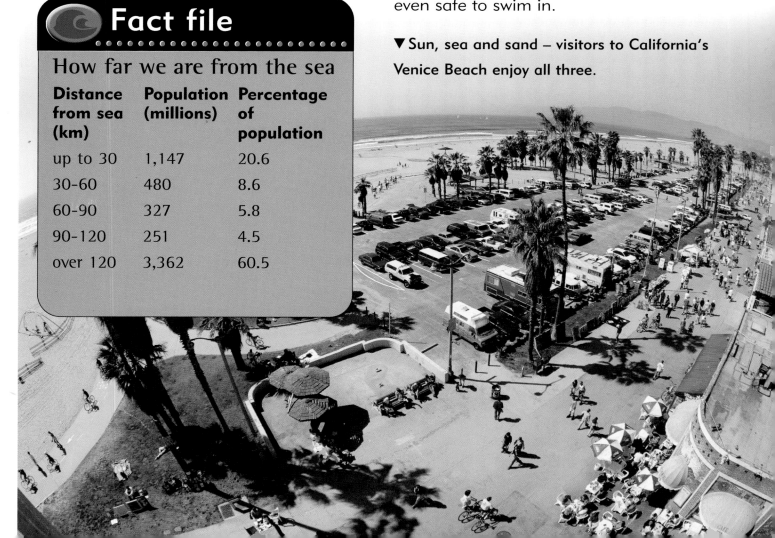

How coasts are formed

Our coastlines have been shaped by powerful forces. If you know what to look for, you can see the traces of earthquakes, volcanoes and great ice ages.

A floating world

Around 250 million years ago, one big sea surrounded one big continent, called Pangaea. Around 200 million years ago, this continent began to break up.

Pangaea was floating like a raft on a layer of super-hot rock or **magma**, inside the Earth. As magma pushed up through cracks in the rock, Pangaea was broken up into separate sections. This happened very slowly, but it never stopped. Between 100 and 50 million years ago, the continents we know today were formed. Earthquakes and volcanoes helped break up the land even more. The continents are still drifting today.

Location file

Ups and downs

The Roman Temple of Serapis at Pozzuoli, Italy, is unusual. Built on dry land, the temple spent hundreds of years under water, before earthquakes forced this coastline up again.

▼ **The coast at Pozzuoli was once underwater.**

Fact file

The Earth takes shape

- 4,550 million years ago – Our planet, the Earth, is formed.
- 3,500 million years ago – The first living things appear on Earth.
- 200 million years ago – Dinosaurs appear; Pangaea breaks up.
- 4 million years ago – Our earliest ancestors appear.
- 100,000 years ago – Modern humans appear.
- 11,000 years ago – The last ice age ends.

The Earth under ice

The Earth's climate can also change land shapes and coastlines. Today's North and South Poles are what remains of the last **ice age** which ended 11,000 years ago. Sheets of ice crept across the continents, flattening plains and gouging out deep valleys. The weight of the ice pushed the land down in many areas. Much of the Earth's water was locked up in the ice. Then when the ice melted, water levels rose suddenly. All these events changed the shape of the world's coasts.

▼ Snow and ice, as here in Antarctica, once covered most of the Earth.

Waves

The sea is never still: waves constantly wash over the shore. These waves may have travelled a long way.

 Location file

Tsunami disaster 2004

On 26 December 2004, an earthquake occurred in the Indian Ocean. Waves reaching 20 m high battered the coasts of Indonesia, India and Sri Lanka. More than 30,000 people were killed. Killer waves also reached East Africa.

Wave formation

Waves are caused by winds as they brush over the surface of the sea. The stronger the wind is, the bigger the waves get. Large waves only build up in great, big oceans; in smaller seas like the Mediterranean, waves are much smaller. Waves flow through water, but they don't move water. Just watch a floating bottle as it bobs up on a passing wave: you'll see that it drops down again exactly where it was before. It does not move in the direction of the wave.

▼ In 1954, Hurricane Carol swept over the whole east coast of the USA. Here a man clings to a tree in New York City.

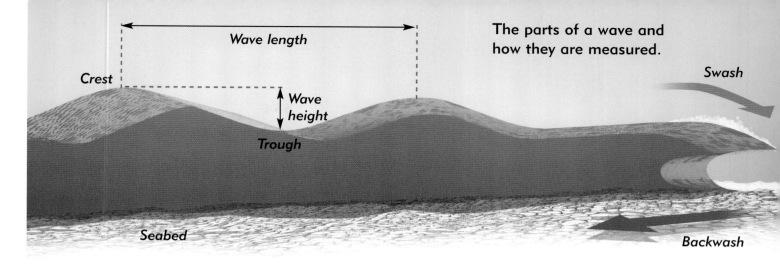

Wave length

Crest

Wave height

Trough

The parts of a wave and how they are measured.

Swash

Seabed

Backwash

When waves reach the shore

In shallow water, the lower part of a wave gets slowed down by brushing against the sand at the bottom. At the same time, the top part of the wave keeps going at the original speed. This is why when a wave reaches the coast, it tumbles forward as if it has just tripped over.

Along oddly shaped coastlines, waves hit the shallows at all sorts of angles. When this happens, the wave changes direction.

Tsunami!

Tsunamis are waves caused by a volcanic eruption or an earthquake. When they reach a coast, these waves can be terrifying.

▼ Without any obstacles in the way, waves crash in at regular intervals.

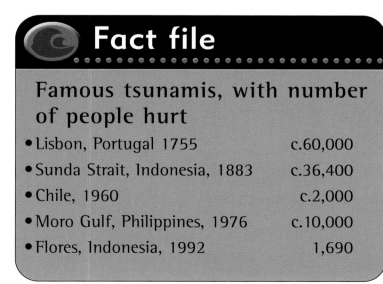

Fact file

Famous tsunamis, with number of people hurt
- Lisbon, Portugal 1755 — c.60,000
- Sunda Strait, Indonesia, 1883 — c.36,400
- Chile, 1960 — c.2,000
- Moro Gulf, Philippines, 1976 — c.10,000
- Flores, Indonesia, 1992 — 1,690

Tides

Long ago, the tides seemed mysterious. Twice each day the level of the ocean would rise and fall. Now we know that the Moon causes tides.

The Moon's effect

Every planet, star and moon in space has **gravity**. Gravity is what pulls other objects closer to each other, like a magnet. The bigger an object is, the stronger its gravity is.

The pull of the Moon's gravity affects the seas on Earth. As it circles the Earth, the Moon's gravity gently pulls the waters of our seas and oceans towards it. The result is what we call tides: the rise and fall of water levels.

Fact file

Tides around the world

The difference between high tide and low tide can be very different depending where you are:

- Bay of Fundy,
  eastern Canada: 16 m
- Avonmouth, England: 15 m
- Seattle, Washington, USA: 3.4 m
- La Coruña, Spain: 2.9 m
- Lowestoft, England: 1.9 m
- Málaga, Spain: 0.84 m
- Galveston, Texas, USA: 0.6 m

▶ A dry harbour at low tide in the Channel Islands, UK.

Special tides

Really high tides happen when the Moon is directly between the Sun and the Earth. The Sun's gravity is added to the Moon's, and makes the tides higher. The smallest tides happen when the pull of the Moon is at right angles to the pull of the Sun.

The more water there is in a sea or ocean, the stronger the Moon's effect is on the tides. The Mediterranean, for example, has small tides. The Gulf of Mexico has only one tide a day instead of two.

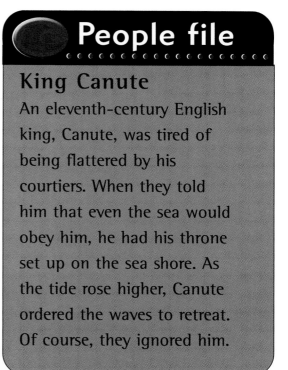

People file

King Canute

An eleventh-century English king, Canute, was tired of being flattered by his courtiers. When they told him that even the sea would obey him, he had his throne set up on the sea shore. As the tide rose higher, Canute ordered the waves to retreat. Of course, they ignored him.

▼ Some power stations use the tides to make electricity. In this **dam**, water at high tide turns **turbines** as it flows back towards the sea.

Currents

The tides and waves are not the only things shaping coastlines. Ocean currents also affect the coastline. Some travel thousands of kilometres.

The Great Conveyor

The network of great oceanic **currents** is often called the Great Conveyor. As they flow around the globe, they change direction and depth. Their movement "stirs" the ocean's waters, transporting oxygen and nutrients.

Most ocean currents are pushed along by winds. In some places, deep ocean currents rise to the surface as they approach a coastline. Large numbers of fish live in these areas because the currents bring food up from the ocean floor.

▼ Sardines mass in their millions off the coast of Natal, South Africa.

Location file

The greatest school on Earth

Warm and cold currents meet off Ilovo Beach, South Africa. Where they meet, the water from the ocean floor rises up, and brings up food for fish from the seabed. Sardines swarm here in staggering numbers every winter to devour the extra food.

The Gulf Stream

The Gulf Stream is an important ocean current. It is a stream of warm water that starts in the Gulf of Mexico and ends in the colder north Atlantic.

Changing direction

Ocean currents are always changing direction, because the world's winds blow in different directions. When they get close to a continent, currents are pushed away. They turn around and start heading in the opposite direction.

▲ A puffin in Scotland's Treshnish Isles – the weather is warmer there, because the waters of the Gulf Stream warm the coast.

▼ In this special photograph, you can see the major ocean currents (yellow, red and white).

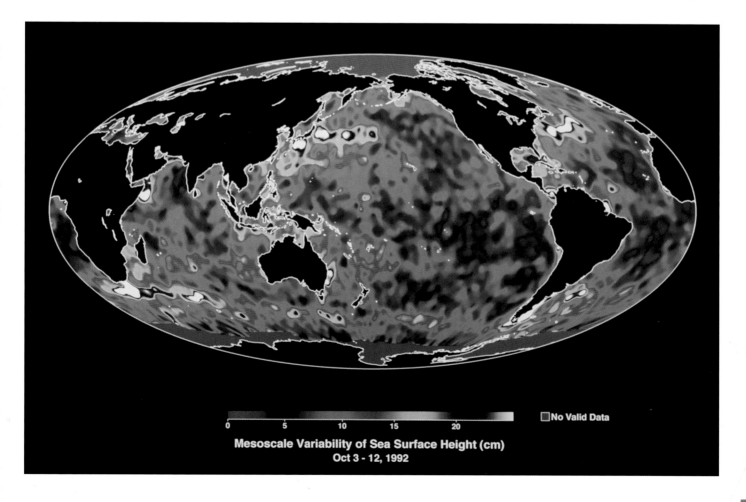

☐ No Valid Data

0   5   10   15   20

Mesoscale Variability of Sea Surface Height (cm)
Oct 3 - 12, 1992

Coastal weather

On a windy winter's day, the coast can seem a very cold place. But actually, places by the sea normally have warmer weather than inland.

Warm winter water

It takes a lot longer to warm water up than rock or earth. It also takes longer for water to cool down. This is why the sea takes longer to warm up in summer than the land. It also takes longer for the sea to cool down in winter. So coasts have warmer winters than inland because the sea keeps them warm.

Sea breezes

During the day, the Sun warms up the air above land quickly. Warm air always rises and cold air always sinks. So when the air above the land becomes warm, it rises up. Cooler air from the sea moves in to replace it. This sea air then gets warmed up too, and so more air moves in from the sea. This makes a breeze.

▼ These drawings show how breezes are made. At night, the pattern is reversed. The land cools quicker than the sea. The breeze then goes in the opposite direction.

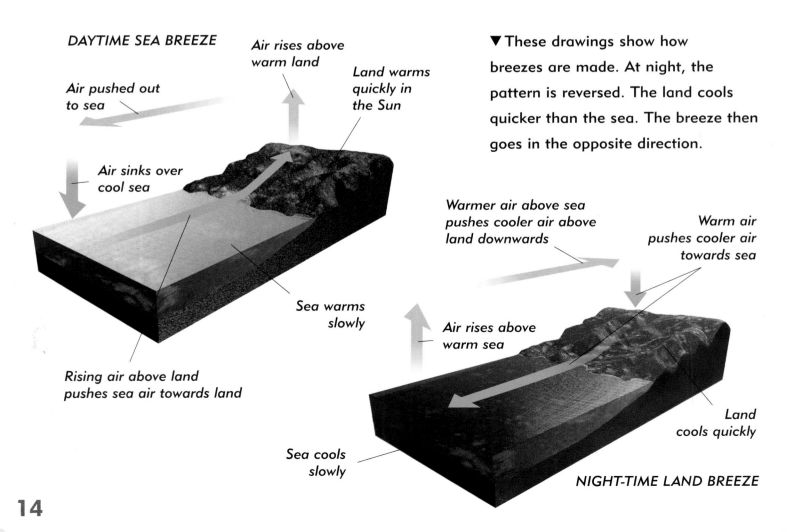

DAYTIME SEA BREEZE

Air rises above warm land

Land warms quickly in the Sun

Air pushed out to sea

Air sinks over cool sea

Sea warms slowly

Rising air above land pushes sea air towards land

Warmer air above sea pushes cooler air above land downwards

Warm air pushes cooler air towards sea

Air rises above warm sea

Land cools quickly

Sea cools slowly

NIGHT-TIME LAND BREEZE

◀ A surfer enjoys a large wave thanks to the coastal breeze which brushes along the surface of the water.

Storms

In **tropical** areas, where the Sun's heat is very strong, breezes can be much stronger and end up as storms. These tropical storms can be very dangerous. When wind speeds are over 119 km per hour, tropical storms are called tropical cyclones.

Fact file

Temperatures for cities on the coast

Compare temperatures for cities inland and on the coast.

	Coldest month (°C)	Warmest month (°C)	Range (°C)
Winnipeg, Canada (inland)	-19	20	39
Seattle, US (coastal)	7	19	12

Location file

Hurricane Mitch

Hurricane Mitch hit Central America's coast in autumn 1998. While terrifying winds blew down buildings and power lines, heavy rains caused floods and landslides. Over 11,000 people died in Honduras and neighbouring Nicaragua.

▶ A young boy stands near what is left of the homes destroyed by Hurricane Mitch.

15

The seashore

1n sunny weather when the sea is warm,
the seaside is a great place to be.
But the sea can also be rough and cold.

Sandy beaches

Sand is made up of broken crystals of **minerals** and crushed seashells. Sand is made by the constant movement of the waves over the beach. Over time, larger pieces of rock are worn smooth. Smaller stones are worn down to around 2 mm, until they become sand.

A raised bump appears where sand piles up at the high-tide line. The land behind this line is known as the backshore. The area that gets covered by the high tide is called the foreshore.

▼ These barriers at Skagen, Denmark make the beach look odd, but they stop the whole coast from being carried away by waves.

Fact file

Sand

Different colours of sand are made up of different minerals. The black beaches of Hawaii and many other Pacific Islands are made from crushed **lava**. The beautiful white beaches of the Caribbean are made from millions of tiny pieces of coral.

The dunes of Jutland

On the coast of Jutland, Denmark, windblown sand forms rolling hills, or dunes. Nearest the sea are mobile dunes, which move very slowly over time. Dunes that have stopped moving have grassed over further inland. Marshy hollows between the dunes are home to natterjack toads.

Longshore drift

Beaches are constantly changing. Some beaches change in a zigzag pattern. This is called longshore drift. It happens when waves hit the coast at an angle. Wave by wave, the sand and stones are slowly moved along the beach. Eventually longshore drift can wash the beach away completely.

Shingle beaches

Shingle or pebble beaches are often steeper than sandy beaches. Waves wash pebbles up onto the beach, but the water trickles through the beached pebbles without dragging them back to the sea.

▼ Fishing boats line the shingle beach at Hastings, on England's southern coast.

The power of waves

Coasts are constantly hit by storms. These wear the coastline away. Every year, storms break off bits of land. Sometimes strange rocks are left.

Taking a pounding

Beaches are important because they protect the land from strong waves. When a strong wave hits a beach, it just moves around sand and pebbles. When there is no beach, the coast gets pounded and slowly wears away.

Where cliffs are made of softer rocks, whole sections of coastline may crumble away in a single storm.

Location file

The Twelve Apostles

The Twelve Apostles (left) of Victoria, Australia, are good examples of the power of waves. These enormous stacks have been shaped by waves over many centuries. Waves are still shaping them today – some of the Apostles have now disappeared!

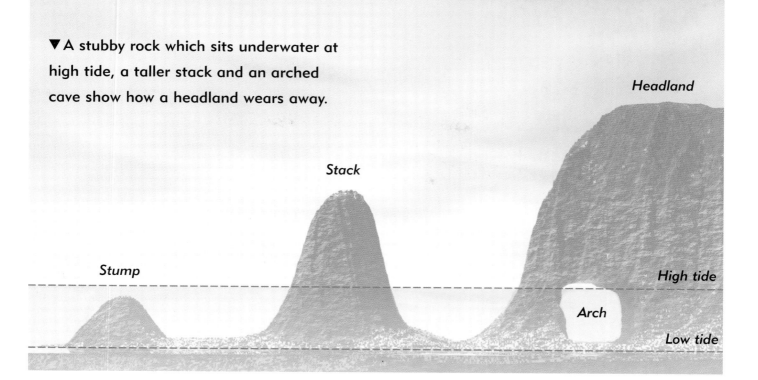

▼ A stubby rock which sits underwater at high tide, a taller stack and an arched cave show how a headland wears away.

Headland

Stack

Stump

High tide

Arch

Low tide

Shaping our coasts

The coasts we see today have all been worn away by waves and storms. Where layers of hard and soft rock lie side by side, they wear away at different speeds. This leaves odd-looking coastlines, with strange shapes in the rock.

Sea sculptures

On some rocky coasts, waves scoop out hollows in the rock. In time, this makes caves or arches in the rock. When the roofs of these arches and caves collapse, towers, called stacks, are left.

▶ You can see the power of the waves as they pound against the rocky coast at Portland Bill, England.

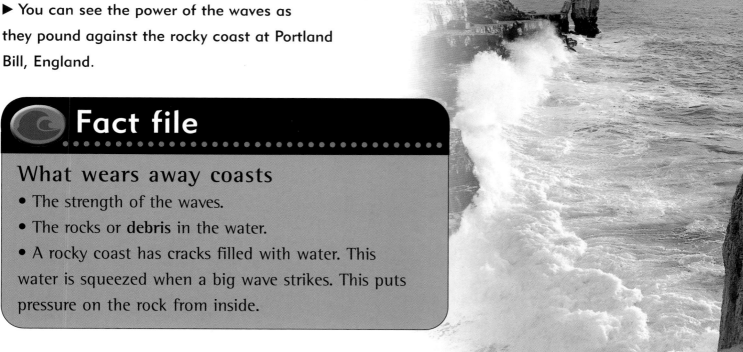

Fact file

What wears away coasts
- The strength of the waves.
- The rocks or **debris** in the water.
- A rocky coast has cracks filled with water. This water is squeezed when a big wave strikes. This puts pressure on the rock from inside.

Building beaches

T he sea can destroy, but it also creates. It builds up areas of coastline. Often it builds a beach in one place with the bits it wore away somewhere else.

Barriers and spits

What is worn away in one place can wash up in another, because of the movement of sand called longshore drift (see page 17). Sometimes the water drops sand or shingle at an angle from the coastline, slowly building up a barrier called a spit. This may grow so long that it cuts right across the mouth of a bay.

Spits also form when the sea water meets a different current – such as a river flowing into the sea. As it hits the flow of the river water, the sea water slows down and the sand it contains drops to the bottom. This forms a spit.

▶ So straight it looks **artificial**, southern England's Chesil Beach is a 30 km spit formed over hundreds of years.

Barrier islands

Over time, spits can grow so much that they become barrier islands. They are flat, low-lying scraps of land. There are many barrier islands along the eastern coast of the USA.

▲ You can see the fringe of barrier islands in this picture of Cape Hatteras in North Carolina, USA.

 Location file

The Wadden Zee

A chain of 23 barrier islands and spits runs along the North Sea coasts of the Netherlands, Germany and southern Denmark, forming a huge **lagoon** called the Wadden Zee. This shallow sea covers over 11,000 km² at high tide.

Coral reefs

Reefs are formed in warm sea water, from the shells of tiny creatures. As generations of corals live and die, their shells pile on top of one another. They form beautiful multi–coloured reefs.

Location file

The Great Barrier Reef

Stretching over 2,000 km up the coast of Queensland, Australia, is the Great Barrier Reef. It is actually a chain of almost 3,000 reefs and home to 400 types of coral, 1,500 types of fish and 4,000 different **molluscs**.

◄ Fish swim in the Great Barrier Reef.

Salt marshes and deltas

Once a river reaches the sea, it slows down. The soil and sand it has been carrying fall to the bottom of the river. The soil and sand pile up and form deltas and mudflats.

Salt marshes

Salt marches form where rivers meet the sea. Few plants can live there, because the tides constantly flood the area with salt water. Plants that do survive there are rewarded with a rich soil that helps them grow.

▼ Mangrove plants growing in a salt marsh. Their roots don't let the salt in.

Special plants

Special plants and shrubs can live in salt marshes. They have found different ways to cope with the salt. They are also used to the changing water level. Some seagrasses survive even though they are covered twice a day, every day.

Mangroves are trees that grow in tropical salt marshes. Many unusual animals live there, such as tree-climbing crabs, mudskipper fish and **aquatic** monkeys.

The Mississippi Delta

The Mississippi Delta covers about a quarter of the entire area of the state of Louisiana, USA. Its rich soils make it perfect for growing crops. The river continues to drop soil there, and this has raised land levels across the delta. Because of this, many old offshoots of the river have been cut off. These offshoots are called bayoux, and they are home to many different plants and animals.

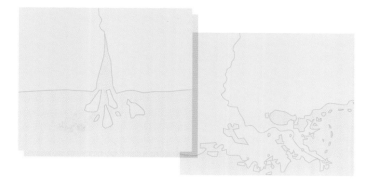

▲ A typical bird's foot delta (above left), and the Mississippi Delta (above right).

▼ A cuspate delta (below left), and the Ganges Delta (below right).

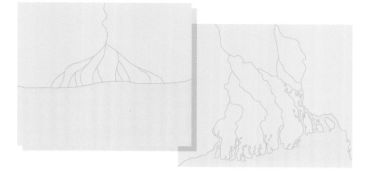

Deltas

If enough mud piles up, it can build up the coastline. The river fans out into lots of little channels as it tries to push through the mud. The result is a delta – named after the ancient Greek letter, which had the same triangular shape.

The world's muddiest rivers

Milligrammes of mud per litre of water.

1	Huang He (Yellow River), China	22,000
2	Nile, Sudan/Egypt	3,700
3	Ganges/Brahmaputra, India/Bangladesh	1,700
4	Purari, Papua New Guinea	1,040
5	Fly, Irian Jaya/Papua New Guinea	390
6	Mississippi, USA	360
7	Mekong, Cambodia/Vietnam	340
8	Po, Italy	325
9	Danube, Central/Eastern Europe	325
10	Yukon, Alaska/Canada	310

▼ Mud from the Yellow River in China brings rich soil to its valley.

Sea animals

Coastal waters are home to many animals, from tiny sea creatures to great sea lions and sharks.

▲ A great white shark tries to catch a seal — which turns out to be a decoy.

Light and life

Why do more animals live in coastal waters than in the deep ocean? One reason is that deep ocean water is very dark. Instead the shallower waters along the coast are lit by the Sun. Plants get plenty of light, and shellfish and corals can live here too. They all provide food and hiding-places for animals like fish, crabs, lobsters and prawns.

 People file

Calypso man

Jacques Cousteau was a famous French diver. Millions of people loved his films. Sailing on his ship, the *Calypso*, he explored the world's oceans. He fought to protect coastlines.

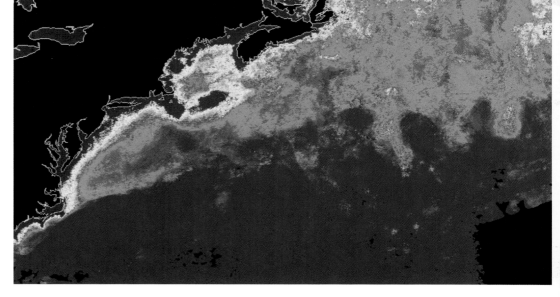

► A satellite photograph shows plankton in the Western Atlantic. The red colour shows where there is the most plankton, off the US coast.

Eat and be eaten

Another reason coastal waters are full of life is that there is so much food. Animal and vegetable remains are carried into the sea by rivers. Currents also bring food up from the deep sea floor when they flow close to coasts.

This food is eaten by **plankton**, tiny sea creatures, and plankton is food for many sea animals, from corals to tiny fish. These tiny fish are eaten by larger fish, which are then eaten by sharks or by sea mammals, such as dolphins or seals.

Location file

Combat coast

Each spring over 8,000 elephant seals come ashore to raise their young at Piedras Blancas, California, USA. First, the males, or bulls, (right) have to fight over the females. Elephant seals get their name from their trunklike nose. The bulls use this nose to make an impressive roar. Over 100,000 tourists come to Piedras Blancas every year to watch them.

► Bull elephant seals fight over females.

A variety of birds

Coastal waters and beaches are home to many different kinds of birds. Each type of bird eats a certain kind of food. Nothing is wasted.

Seabird cities

Large **colonies** of seabirds nest on coastal cliffs around the world. Others live on strips of coast and small islands. These colonies are like cities, not only because they are big, but also because so many different birds live so close together. Like cities, seabird colonies have many dangers. Gangs of gulls can snatch unguarded eggs or steal young chicks. Skuas can chase smaller fishing birds and terrify them into throwing up their food.

▶ This sheer cliff is home to a colony of kittiwakes.

26

A world of waders

Waders are birds that live on sandy beaches and mudflats. They have long legs to paddle through the shallows, and long beaks to search the sand for food. Waders often flock in their thousands. They are often difficult to tell apart, since they are coloured to fit in with their sandy surroundings. But they have many different designs of beak that can point, probe, flip pebbles or skim the sand in search of food.

Fact file

Australian waders: all kinds of beaks

- **Eastern Curlew** Very long (up to 18 cm), curved, thin, that can feel, for searching for worms and tiny crabs.
- **Bar-tailed Godwit** Long, slightly upward-curling, with a flexible tip for rummaging in the sand.
- **Red Knot** Straight beak. Short but strong.
- **Ruddy Turnstone** Short, thick and strong at the base, for turning over small stones.

Location file

Pasir Ris Park

Near Singapore is a city park with a difference: it is right in the middle of a mangrove swamp. Along with swings, slides and grassy lawns, there are more unusual attractions, like exotic seasnakes, mudskipper fish and fiddler crabs.

▶ A flock of lesser flamingoes graces the coast of Namibia, at Walvis Bay.

Living by the sea

You can find food on the land and in the sea. In the past, people had to find food close to home, so it made sense to live near the land and the sea.

The world's first rubbish

Our early ancestors lived by the sea. At the mouth of the Klasies River, in South Africa, a 100,000-year-old rubbish dump has been found. The rubbish is very important, because it can tell us how our ancestors lived and what they ate.

▼ **An Inuit hunts in the Arctic with a harpoon.**

The ancient rubbish tells us that our ancestors looked both inland and out to sea for food. The shells of mussels, clams and limpets left there show that the people ate seafood, though they don't seem to have had nets or poles for fishing. There are also penguin and seal bones, as well as antelope and buffalo. So we know they ate food from the land and from the sea.

Location file

The sands of time

Just north of Liverpool, England, Formby Beach has long been a popular tourist attraction. But a shift in the tides has uncovered traces of human and animal footprints, baked hard in the mud by the Sun 6,000 years ago.

People file

Dished up whale

In 1805 the Lewis and Clark expedition across North America reached the Pacific. Kallamuck Indians they met there offered them some whale. 'I had a part of it cooked and found it very palatable and tender,' wrote Captain Lewis.

▲ Istanbul's position on the busy waters between Europe and Asia has made it an important city for many centuries.

Protecting coasts

The sea can be dangerous. Coastal flooding has killed many people and damaged large areas of land. People are always trying to find ways of protecting their homes.

Disappearing coasts

Some 70 per cent of the world's sandy beaches are now being worn away. If the problem gets worse, it will mean disaster for many tourist spots. It is even tougher for people who live on clifftops, who can lose their homes when coasts wear away.

Beating a retreat

Not much can be done to help people whose houses are about to collapse into the sea. Experts think that the best thing is to let the sea break down the land in some places and then build it up in others.

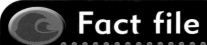 **Fact file**

Defence solutions

- **Sea Walls** Made of concrete; they work, but they cost a lot to build and keep.
- **Groynes** Low walls that stick out from the shore.
- **Gabions** Wire baskets packed with large rocks. They work, but cost a lot and are ugly.
- **Revetments** Low wooden barriers along a beach or the base of a cliff. Ugly and fragile.

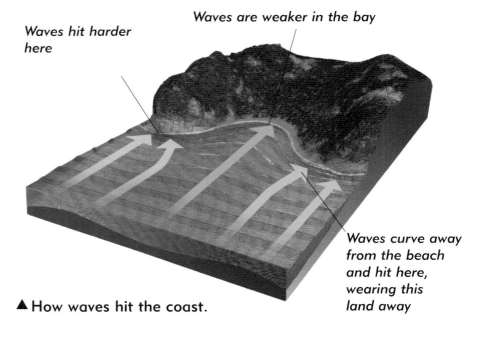

Waves hit harder here

Waves are weaker in the bay

Waves curve away from the beach and hit here, wearing this land away

▲ How waves hit the coast.

▶ A homeowner watches helplessly as seawater surges into his sitting room.

▲ Chestertown, Maryland, USA after Hurricane Frederick, in 1979.

Making a stand

Sometimes – when whole towns or important roads are in danger, for example – the sea has to be held back. One way of doing this is to pile new sand or stone on the beach. Another way is to build walls.

Artificial reefs, built up to 5 km offshore, may be a better way. These barriers can even be built from old tyres. They break up waves and weaken them. Other solutions include artificial islands and barriers that stand out at right angles from the shore. These also help break up waves. The problem is that any barrier that protects one coastline makes the problem worse somewhere else.

Location file

Narrowneck

The beach at Gold Coast, Queensland, Australia, has been badly worn away. This is a problem for tourism and for parts of the city that could be flooded. Now an artificial reef, known as Narrowneck or Nazz, built from sandbags 150 m offshore, is protecting the coastline. But it has also helped make bigger and better waves for the surfers now flocking to Gold Coast.

31

Pleasant coasts

In some countries, coasts are the only places where people can live. Coasts offer flat land, mild weather and rich soil for crops.

The first Australians

The interior of Australia is mostly desert. So when the first Aborigines arrived in Australia, 50,000 years ago, their first settlements were along the coast. Over generations they moved further inland. They found ways of surviving in the desert.

▼ A canal, on the right, brings life–saving water to fields in Algeria.

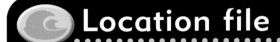

Location file

Algeria

Over 80 per cent of Algeria is in the Sahara Desert. The rest of the country is in the Atlas Mountains. Only 6 per cent of the country's land can be used to grow crops. This land is a thin strip just 20–80 km wide along the coast of the Mediterranean. Here, Algeria's farmers grow wheat, dates, olives and citrus fruits, and keep herds of cattle.

▲ Sydney's suburbs hug the coast.
Most Australians live close to the sea.

European ideas

The first European settlers in Australia
had different ideas. The newcomers
were farmers. Any land not used for
farming was considered useless.
Europeans preferred the land along the
coast because it was flat, had good
weather and good soil. It was also much
easier to build roads and railways along
the coast than over mountains or
through deserts.

 Location file

The Atacama Desert

The world's driest desert is the
Atacama Desert in Chile. It lies
between the Pacific Ocean and the
Andes Mountains. This coastal area
is extremely dry. It rains once every
100 years here.

Ports and shipping

For centuries the sea was the only way to travel long distances. Today, many things are still sent by ship.

Shipping – then and now

Once, people who wished to trade across the seas had to go by ship. Today goods – and people – can go by aeroplane. Even so, transporting large things by sea is cheaper than by air.

▼ For 200 years, New York City welcomed generations of European immigrants who arrived by boat.

Ships still trade back and forth across the world's oceans. Refrigerated ships bring meat, fruit and vegetables. Giant supertankers carry fuel. Smaller ships carry cooking oils, like soya or olive oil. There are even ships that specialize in transporting wine.

▲ Containers are stacked up on docks, waiting
to continue their journey by ship or by road.

Containers

Container shipping has become popular in
the last thirty years. Goods are packed in
metal containers which are moved quickly and
easily from one form of transport to another.
A container may start its journey on a truck
or a train, and then may be lifted onto a ship.
When the ship arrives in the next country, the
container can be put on another truck.

For short sea-crossings, ro-ro (roll-on, roll-off)
ferries let trucks and cars simply drive onboard
in one port, and drive off again at another.

Fact file

Top 10 world ports
(by tons of products transported, 2003)

1 Singapore
2 Rotterdam, Netherlands
3 South Louisiana, USA
4 Shanghai, China
5 Hong Kong, China
6 Houston, USA
7 Chiba, Japan
8 Nagoya, Japan
9 Ulsan, South Korea
10 Kwangyang, South Korea

Sailing safely

Long stretches of coast may be very dangerous to ships and boats. Lighthouses, radar and satellites are all used to help avoid shipwrecks.

Lighthouses

Lighthouses have been used since ancient times to warn ships of dangerous coastlines. The Pharos, or lighthouse, at Alexandria, Egypt, was a wonder of the ancient world. Today lighthouses use the latest lightbulbs and special mirrors. Their light can be seen many kilometres away, in any weather. With **radar** and radio, coastguards can contact boats if they see them wandering off-course.

Today satellites help a ship's crew to work out where they are to within a few metres, and **sonar** warns them of unexpected shallow water. Ships' captains read charts that show where rocks or sandbanks are. **Buoys** are attached to the bottom of the sea and float on the water above. They help guide ships around dangerous spots.

 Location file

The not-so-light house

Built in the 1870s, the world's tallest brick lighthouse is North Carolina's Cape Hatteras Lighthouse. It weighs over 4,000 tonnes. But the lighthouse was built on sand which was steadily wearing away. In 1999, engineers began work on the building. Using a special steel track, they moved the lighthouse to another place almost a kilometre away on higher ground.

◀ A busy dock in Brazil. Trade is important all along Brazil's Atlantic coast.

▲ A sailor carefully plots his ship's course through coastal waters.

Dredging

Sometimes shallow coastal waters need to be deepened so ships can sail safely along them. Dredgers are special ships that can scoop up sand from the bottom or suck it up like a vacuum cleaner. Today's supertankers and container ships are very big and need plenty of depth, otherwise they can get stuck.

 Fact file

Historic shipwrecks

- c.1300 BCE A Syrian trader wrecked off Cape Gelidonya, Turkey.
- c.80 BCE A Roman ship sank off the island of Antikythera, Greece, carrying a strange machine that some people think was an early computer.
- 1545 Henry VIII's warship, the *Mary Rose*, sank off southern England.
- 1622 A Spanish treasure fleet was wrecked in the Straits of Florida.

Fishing

Fishing has been a way of life for people living on the coast for thousands of years. Today, fishing has become big business.

Location file

The divers of Cheju

The *haenyo* divers of Cheju, South Korea, have a 1,500 year history. These women dive to depths of up to 25 m for minutes at a time in search of shellfish. But times have changed, and fewer people want to do such dangerous work. In the 1930s there were over 20,000 *haenyo*; today there are only 3,000.

Making a living

For thousands of years, fishermen have lived on the coast. But today, traditional fishermen catch fewer fish. They have to compete with fleets of foreign **trawlers** and giant factory-ships.

▶ Modern fishing methods catch enormous amounts of fish.

▼ A Burmese fisherman works in the traditional way.

The three main fishing nets used today.

Drift net

Purse seine

Trawl

Fact file

Know your nets

- **Seine** Square with weights around the edges so it folds inward. It is a traditional net.
- **Purse seine** Large enough to catch an entire school of fish, and big enough to hold a cathedral.
- **Trawl** A big bag held open at the mouth, and drawn behind a boat; some trawls are big enough to swallow a dozen jumbo jets!
- **Drift** Widely banned, drift nets are weighted at the bottom but buoyed up at the top to form a wall that can be up to 10 km long.

Overfishing

Today fishing is big business, with huge catches that make a lot of money. In fifty years, the total number of fish caught in the world has quadrupled.

This can't continue. Already, Canada has had to close cod fisheries because there are not enough fish any more. The same thing is happening in the North Sea. Tuna catches in the West Atlantic are a twelfth of what they were thirty years ago. In rich countries, many people are losing their jobs. In poorer countries, fish is a very important source of food. Without fish, people will go hungry.

Seaside holidays

Many people have beach holidays at least once a year. People often visit the seaside for a weekend, or even just for a day trip.

Seaside holidays

When people began working in factories in the 1800s and offices in the 1900s, seaside holidays suddenly became popular. When the first railways were built in the 1800s, it was easier to go to the seaside. Thousands of people flocked to the new seaside resorts.

In the 1900s more people started to drive cars. Cars were sometimes advertised as a way of getting to the seaside.

▼ Hotels and villas surround a beach full of holidaymakers in the summer.

People file

Thomas Cook

Born in the English Midlands, Thomas Cook was a Baptist missionary. He preached the importance of a holy life and temperance (not drinking alcohol). It was for a temperance meeting that, in 1841, he organized his first railway trip from Leicester to Loughborough. In ten years he arranged more trips, building up the world's first travel agency.

Flying south for the winter

Aeroplanes meant people could go further away. By the 1960s, northern Europeans were flying south to the Spanish coast, drawn by cheap prices and guaranteed sunshine.

Tailor-made tourism

Over time people began to feel they were being crammed by the thousands into identical hotels in identical resorts. Some people began looking for more interesting holidays, with everything from whale-watching to jet-skiing and scuba-

diving. Young backpackers travelled farther afield in search of fun and adventure, exploring coasts from Brazil to Bali, from South Africa to Thailand.

▼ A Filipino fishing town celebrates the whale shark. Once they hunted these giant, harmless sharks. Now they work as guides for tourists.

Coasts in danger

Our coasts are often very beautiful, but they are also very fragile. Today, building on coastlines, watersports and pollution are damaging them.

Damaging coasts

Thousands of kilometres of coastline around the world have been covered over by big hotels and resorts. Whether you visit the Seychelles, Mexico, or the Red Sea coast of Egypt, these large tourist resorts often look the same. Resorts can bring jobs and money, but sand dunes, salt marshes, coral reefs and mangrove swamps are all destroyed to build them.

Container ports, roads, apartments, golf courses, theme parks and many other attractions damage coastlines. Some coasts are now protected. For example, the California Coastal Act of 1976 limited construction on coasts in that state.

Fact file

Sources of sea pollution
- Sewage and industrial waste are often pumped straight into the sea.
- Chemicals like fertilisers and weedkillers are washed into streams and rivers by rain, then carried into the sea.
- Air pollution, in smoke or fumes, ends up in the sea when it rains.

▼ A beautiful golf course – but was it once a home for animals and birds?

Pollution

In rich countries, it is now unusual for factories to pour out smoke or dump chemicals into the ocean, like they used to. But some businesses are still caught causing pollution, and accidents can happen. Even a small accident can poison the countryside and be harmful to people.

Factories in poorer countries are less controlled. It costs a lot to check if factories are obeying the law. Poorer countries also complain that the world's rich countries got rich while causing pollution. Sometimes big companies dump dangerous chemicals in poor countries.

▲ Coastal buildings and businesses can be a form of pollution.

Location file

Galicia

In November 2002, an old oil tanker, the *Prestige*, sank off Galicia, in Spain. Thousands of tonnes of oil leaked out. Several hundred kilometres of coastline were polluted, covering tourist beaches and seabird colonies and destroying 21,500 jobs in Galicia's fishing industry. Most of the oil in the tanker sank with it to the bottom. The remaining oil was taken out of the tanker in 2004.

◀ Volunteers help clean up after the *Prestige* disaster.

A world underwater?

Recently people have become worried about global warming. This will cause sea levels to rise. If they do rise, many coastal areas could end up under water.

Global warming?

Sea levels have always risen and fallen. So we know that today's coastlines will not be there forever.

This natural pattern may change in the future because of global warming. Global warming is caused by pollution that ends up in the Earth's atmosphere and traps heat from the Sun, causing what is called the Greenhouse Effect. The Earth becomes like a giant greenhouse, keeping all the heat inside that could escape into space. A warmer world causes ice and snow at the North and South Poles to melt and so sea levels will rise.

But not everyone agrees that sea level rises will be so awful. Experts disagree about how much the level of the seas will rise.

Location file

The Marshall Islands

Only a few of the 34 Marshall Islands rise much more than 2.5 m above the ocean. If sea levels were to rise by half a metre, life for the islanders would become very difficult. The entire islands would not be under water, but storm waves and high tides might damage farmland and fresh water. A series of floods has already forced some islanders to leave their homes for higher ground. Many people will have to leave the islands for good.

▼ A California farm is almost completely underwater after floods.

People file

Jean Baptiste Fourier

Jean Baptiste Fourier, the man who first thought of the Greenhouse Effect, was born in France in 1768. Fourier was a famous mathematician. In 1827 he wrote about how the Earth's atmosphere could keep heat from escaping into space.

◀ Even airborne pollution ends up in the sea, carried by rainfall and rivers.

▶ A factory in Shanghai, China, pours out pollution.

Glossary

Aquatic Something that lives in water.

Artificial Made by people.

Buoys Floating coloured markers that are anchored to the bottom of the sea. They warn ships that there are dangers hidden under the surface of the water, such as rocks and shallows.

Colony An area where a type of animal or plant lives together in large numbers.

Current A strong stream of water that moves in a specific direction.

Dam A wall built across a river or stream that holds the water back.

Debris The bits left over when something is broken up.

Dune A mound of sand.

Gravity The Earth's gravity is what gives us weight and stops us floating off the ground.

Ice age A long period of time when the Earth's temperature is lower than it is now and sheets of ice cover much of the planet.

Lagoon A small area of water that is cut off from the sea.

Lava Hot molten rock that comes to the surface, often in volcanic eruptions.

Magma The deep layer of super-hot rock that lies under the Earth's solid crust; when it seeps out to the surface it is known as lava.

Mangrove A tree that grows along tropical coasts with its roots anchored in mud.

Minerals Natural materials that form crystals. Sulphur, gold, silver, copper and diamond are all kinds of minerals.

Mollusc An animal that lives in water. Many have an external shell or have internal shells that serve as skeletons. Clams, oysters, mussels, snails, slugs, octopuses and squid are all molluscs.

Plankton Tiny animals and plants that float in sea water.

Radar A way of using radio waves to find out the position of things.

Sonar A way of using sound waves to find objects under water.

Trawlers A boat that drags a trawl net behind it to catch fish.

Tropical An area on the Earth, near the Equator, that is always warm and wet.

Turbine A spinning motor that is driven by water or steam to make electricity.

Further information

Websites to visit

www.timeforkids.com/TFK/specials/
articles/0,6709,1113542,00.html
Time magazine's children's page
explains how polar ice is melting due
to global warming.

http://www.nationalgeographic.com/
earthpulse/reef/reef1_flash-feature.html
Discover the animals that live in the
beautiful Great Barrier Reef on the
site of the famous *National
Geographic* magazine.

Books to read

Mapping Earthforms: Coasts by Catherine
Chambers and Nicholas Lapthorn
(Heinemann Library, 2007).

Earth's Changing Coasts by Neil Morris
(Raintree 2004).

*Earth's Changing Landscape: Changing
Coastlines* by Philip Steele (Smart Apple
Media, 2004).

Our Planet in Peril: Global Warming by
Chris Oxlade (Franklin Watts, 2002).

Index